Who Is My Neighbor?

Christopher J. Ruff, M.A., S.T.L.

Who Is My Neighbor?

Novo Millennio Press
PO Box 160
La Crescent, MN 55947
www.novomill.com

Nihil obstat: Rev. Samuel A. Martin, S.T.L.
Censor Librorum

Imprimatur: Jerome E. Listecki, D.D., J.C.D.
Bishop of La Crosse
October 1, 2009

The *nihil obstat* and *imprimatur* are official declarations that a book or pamphlet is free of doctrinal or moral error. No implication is contained therein that those who have granted the *nihil obstat* and *imprimatur* agree with the contents, opinions, or statements expressed.

Cover art:
Kathleen Bausch, *Christ the Good Samaritan,* 2008.
Used by permission of Catholic Charities of the Diocese of La Crosse. All rights reserved.

Graphics and Design:
Alice J. Andersen
www.alicejandersen.com.

A Resource for
Small Group Faith Sharing

The Discipleship Series

Novo Millennio Press

Foreword

In the summer of 2006, Christopher Ruff, director of the Office of Ministries and Social Concerns for our diocese, came to me with a proposal. He wanted to develop a diocesan small group faith-sharing program that would take the typical "Bible study" ingredients of prayer, reflective study and fellowship, and add one more—loving service.

Chris felt too many Catholics saw ministry to the suffering and needy as belonging only to Church social justice committees and institutions like Catholic Charities, with their own role reduced to giving these groups financial support. Of course, it is true that Jesus tells the story of a Samaritan who gave money to an innkeeper for the care of a beaten man—but not before compassion had moved the Samaritan personally to clean the man's wounds with oil and wine and to lift him onto his own animal to bring him to that inn.

With this kind of love of neighbor in mind, Chris looked for a faith-sharing resource that would combine a prayerful, contemplative spirit with the universal call to serve Christ in "the least of his brethren." He wanted to find something that penetrated to the heart of the Gospel but that was concise, readable and workable for people with busy lives. Even the vital service component had to be manageable and broad enough to include various kinds of service. In the end, Chris decided to write his own resource, on his own time so he could publish it. He then wrote a second and a third book, and continues to develop more.

The response in the Diocese of La Crosse has been extraordinary. In what was supposed to be a small pilot phase in Lent of 2007, over one thousand people in more than thirty parishes took part (in our modest Wisconsin diocese of 165 parishes). Concluding surveys reflected great enthusiasm and more than 95% said they wished to continue with the next resource. As the program was made available to the entire diocese with the second book, nearly two thousand people joined groups in close to one hundred parishes. This enthusiastic response has continued year by year as the program has become firmly rooted and indeed spread to other dioceses.

This expanding set of faith-sharing resources is aptly named the Discipleship Series. I am seeing it form disciples in our diocese—integral and authentic disciples growing in love of God and love of neighbor. It is my hope that in the planting and nurturing brought about through this Discipleship Series, we will look forward to a harvest of apostolic works. I recommend it wholeheartedly to individuals, groups, parishes and other dioceses that wish to foster a deeper discipleship in Christ.

Most Rev. Jerome E. Listecki
Bishop of La Crosse

Acknowledgments

I would like to express my gratitude to Bishop Jerome Listecki for his enthusiastic support of this project at every phase, both within and beyond the Diocese of La Crosse.

I would like to acknowledge Deacon Stephen Najarian, who first awakened me to the idea that faith-sharing groups should have a component of service, and Deacon Richard Sage, whose witness of care for the poor and the marginalized as Executive Director of Catholic Charities of the Diocese of La Crosse has been an inspiration.

I also want to thank Alice Andersen for her skilled editing and design.

Finally, I voice my deepest gratitude to my wife Clare for her continued patience with my late nights at the keyboard.

Christopher Ruff

Table of Contents

Introduction

Welcome to *Who Is My Neighbor,* part of the Discipleship Series of faith-sharing resources.

As with other books in this series, the focus is different from "Bible studies" that take a more linear and academic approach.

Our focus in this book is to:

- Soak deeply and prayerfully in a small, select number of Gospel passages;
- See the meaning of those passages come alive in human stories that inspire;
- Reflect as a small group on discussion questions that apply to daily living;
- Foster a modest commitment to love of neighbor through service;
- Experience in our hearts the fullness of joy that only Christ can give!

In over twenty years of organizing and writing materials for faith-sharing groups, these are the fruits I have come to see and expect. The component of active love of neighbor comes from the conviction that true discipleship must take seriously Jesus' words, "Whatever you did for the least of my brethren, you did for me" (Mt 25:40). And truly the fruit of love is joy—*a warm, inspired joy that I have seen blossom over and over again as a result of this faith-sharing experience.*

As support for this approach, consider Jesus' allegory of the Vine and the branches (John 15:1-17). We have all heard it many times, with its image of Jesus as the Vine, to whom we as branches must be joined if we are to bear fruit. I encourage you to read it again and to reflect on some key phrases:

"Abide in me...abide in my love."

Let "...my words abide in you."

"...that you bear much fruit, and so prove to be my disciples."

"Love one another as I have loved you."

"...that my joy may be in you, and that your joy may be full."

(see verses 4-12)

I believe we can find in these forty-six words of Jesus the very essence of his Gospel, his call to us. And the faith-sharing approach of the Discipleship Series is an attempt to respond actively and enthusiastically to that call. *"Abiding" bears fruit in love, whose nectar is joy.*

A word about the icon on the cover of this book. It is the work of artist Kathleen Bausch and was donated to

Catholic Charities of the Diocese of La Crosse for use on materials for its Good Samaritan Affiliates. The affiliates unite their daily prayers, sacrifices and acts of love with the work of Catholic Charities, seen as an expression of the compassion of Christ. Deacon Richard Sage, Executive Director of Catholic Charities of the Diocese of La Crosse, gave kind permission for the image to be used on the cover of this book. The icon beautifully conveys the spirit and goals of the Discipleship Series by showing that it is first of all Christ who is the Good Samaritan, the one who ministers to us in our weak and fallen condition so that we may then, in union with him, touch the lives of our brothers and sisters in need.

Let us, then, listen and abide. And may the fruit of our abiding be a fuller, more charitable, more joyful discipleship that moves the world to marvel, as the ancient pagans did: "See how they love one another!"

Christopher Ruff

How to Use This Book

The Discipleship Series of faith-sharing materials aims to be simple and flexible. What follows is everything you need to know to move forward:

Establishing and Running One or More Groups

- Form one or more small groups (5-12 people each) through personal invitation or parish announcements. For customizable bulletin inserts/flyers, visit www.novomill.com and click on "Parish Launch Kit."

- If established for Lent, the groups should meet weekly. Otherwise, once a month tends to be more workable for most people's schedules. Typical length for a session is about 90 minutes. Whatever time frame is established, it should be rigorously respected.

- Each group should have a facilitator. It can be the same person at each meeting, or the facilitator role can rotate.

- The job of the facilitator is not to be an expert in the material or to do a lot of talking. Rather, it is to start and end the meeting on time, to help keep things moving and on topic, and to foster a friendly, supportive environment in which everyone feels invited to contribute.

- The group members decide where they would
  like to meet. It is ideal to hold the sessions in
  each other's homes since a key goal is to bring
  faith into daily life. If this is not workable, a
  room on church grounds is fine, or some com-
  bination of the two.

- Each member is expected to read the material prayerfully ahead of the session, jotting
  a few notes in response to the "Questions for
  Discussion."

- The session begins with the Prayer to the
  Holy Spirit or some other appropriate prayer
  so that hearts may be opened to God's presence.

- It is strongly recommended that the group
  members then read aloud the material for
  that session, taking turns reading a few para-
  graphs or a small section. This pattern should
  continue all the way through the discussion
  questions. Experience has shown this reading
  aloud to be not only do-able (within a 90-min-
  ute time frame), but quite fruitful, making
  the material fresh and alive.

- When there are about ten minutes left in
  the allotted schedule, it is time to proceed to
  the "Group Prayers of Intercession," even if
  the group has not finished all the discussion
  questions.

- The prayers of intercession are intended to be spontaneous prayer intentions. They direct the power of prayer to various needs and simultaneously deepen the spirit of fellowship in the group. Conclude with the "Closing Prayer."

- The session should end on time, even if members are eager to keep going. This is vital for the health and longevity of the group. It is good to follow with fifteen or twenty minutes of social time for those who are able to stay. Simple refreshments are a nice touch, with emphasis on the word simple; otherwise, people feel pressure to keep up with high expectations.

The Service Component

- The Service Component distinguishes this program from many other faith-sharing approaches. It is anticipated that group members will devote an hour or two to some form of service between sessions (if meetings are weekly, this could be an hour or two each month). The service may be carried out individually or together with others.

- Service can take many forms, but it should come from the heart. Certainly service to the poor, the sick, the elderly, the homebound, the homeless, etc., has always had a privileged place for Christ's followers.

- Some may already be devoting a great deal of time to service. In that case, it is enough to consciously "dedicate" some portion of that service to the group's communal effort and spirit.

- Each set of "Questions for Discussion" includes at least one that touches on the component of service. This is to keep alive the awareness of the importance of the service aspect, which however is done on the "honor system" (with no one watching over anyone else's shoulder).

Group Etiquette

- Pray for the members of your group between sessions.

- Maintain confidentiality.

- Be a good listener and encourage everyone to contribute to the discussion, without anyone monopolizing. Members that are more talkative should allow everyone a chance to respond before they speak a second time.

- Love your neighbor by speaking charitably and refraining from any kind of gossip.

- Be on time, come prepared, and actively take part in discussion and prayer.

- Take seriously the service component so that you may be a loving (and always humble) witness to the others in your group.

- Be open and expect God's action in your life and prayer—expect to be changed!

Recommended prayer to start each session:

Prayer to the Holy Spirit

**Come Holy Spirit,
Fill our hearts with the fire of your love.**

**Draw us near to Jesus,
so that we may witness to his presence
in every moment of our lives.**

**Renew us, so that our homes, parishes,
neighborhoods and world
may be transformed into the heavenly
Father's kingdom on earth,
where love and mercy reign.**

Amen.

Session 1

Who Is My Neighbor?

The Lord in His Scriptures

The Parable of the Good Samaritan

And behold, a lawyer stood up to put him to the test, saying, "Teacher, what shall I do to inherit eternal life?" He said to him, "What is written in the law? How do you read?" And he answered, "You shall love the Lord your God with all your heart, and with all your soul, and with all your strength, and with all your mind; and your neighbor as yourself." And he said to him, "You have answered right; do this, and you will live."

But he, desiring to justify himself, said to Jesus, "And who is my neighbor?"

Jesus replied, "A man was going down from Jerusalem to Jericho, and he fell among robbers, who stripped

him and beat him, and departed, leaving him half dead.
Now by chance a priest was going down that road; and
when he saw him he passed by on the other side. So
likewise a Levite, when he came to the place and saw
him, passed by on the other side. But a Samaritan, as he
journeyed, came to where he was; and when he saw him,
he had compassion, and went to him and bound up his
wounds, pouring on oil and wine; then he set him on his
own beast and brought him to an inn, and took care of
him. And the next day he took out two denarii and gave
them to the innkeeper, saying, 'Take care of him; and
whatever more you spend, I will repay you when I come
back.' Which of these three, do you think, proved neighbor
to the man who fell among the robbers?"

He said, "The one who showed mercy on him." And
Jesus said to him, "Go and do likewise."
Luke 10:25-37.

Soak in the Word

Two Minutes of Silence

Reflect...

This would have been a shocking parable to Jewish ears, for the Jews detested the Samaritans and regarded them as heretics. Samaritans felt the same about the Jews. This mutual hatred stemmed from Old Testament times, when the Assyrians captured the district of Samaria and deported most of the Israelites, leaving the remaining Jews to intermarry with non-Jewish peoples. The result was a mixed race with mixed religious beliefs that differed from the Jewish faith in a number of ways. The most notable difference was the chief place of worship, which for the Jews was Jerusalem with its Temple, but for the Samaritans was Mt. Gerizim, where Moses commanded the blessings of the law to be proclaimed (see Deuteronomy 11:23; 27:12-13).

Fully aware of this legacy of mutual hatred, Jesus tells this parable in which a Jewish man beaten and left for dead by robbers receives no mercy from a priest and a Levite who share his Jewish faith, but is show tremendous compassion by a passing Samaritan.

Why do the priest and the Levite pass by? Their roles involved sacred functions associated with worship and the Temple, and to touch a dead body was to be rendered "unclean" or unholy (see Leviticus 21:1-4). A good priest could not even take the risk of investigating to see whether the "half dead" man was still alive or not.

Jesus is showing that such an attachment to externals and to ritual purity ends up being an obstacle to the practice of love of neighbor. It is the Samaritan who steps in and shows a superabundance of love, cleaning the victim's wounds with oil and wine, lifting him onto his animal (leaving himself to walk), and paying for his care at an inn.

Jesus' message is that there are no special criteria that make other people my neighbors. No, it is I who must make *myself* neighbor to *them,* to anyone and everyone, especially if they are in need. And it is not just a matter of sweet sentiments—no, it must engage me in actions of love on their behalf.

Pope John Paul II

Everyone who stops beside the suffering of another person, whatever form it may take, is a Good Samaritan. This stopping does not mean curiosity but availability. It is like the opening of a certain interior disposition of the heart, which also has an emotional expression of its own. The name "Good Samaritan" fits every individual who is sensitive to the sufferings of others, who "is moved" by the misfortune of another.

Nevertheless, the Good Samaritan of Christ's parable does not stop at sympathy and compassion alone. They become for him an incentive to actions aimed at bringing help to the injured man. In a word, then, a Good Samaritan is one who brings help in suffering, whatever its nature may be. Help which is, as far as possible, effective. He puts his whole heart into it, nor does he spare material means.

Following the parable of the Gospel, we could say that suffering, which is present under so many different forms in our human world, is also present in order to unleash love in the human person, that unselfish gift of one's "I" on behalf of other people, especially those who suffer. The world of human suffering unceasingly calls for, so to speak, another world: the world of human love; and in a certain sense man owes to suffering that unselfish love which stirs in his heart and actions.

(On the Christian Meaning of Human Suffering, **nn. 28-29)**

Catechism of the Catholic Church

1932 - The duty of making oneself a neighbor to others and actively serving them becomes even more urgent when it involves the disadvantaged, in whatever area this may be. "As you did it to one of the least of these my brethren, you did it to me."[1]

---

[1]Mt 25:40.

The Lord in the Life of His People

"A Light is Shining in the Poor"

If one asks who has embodied the spirit of the Good Samaritan in our day, Blessed Mother Teresa of Calcutta comes immediately to mind, and for good reason. But another figure, though not as universally known, has also given an extraordinary witness in this way. He is Jean Vanier, and what follows is a glimpse into a life dedicated to love.

It is a crisp October day on the wooded campus of St. John's University in Collegeville, Minnesota. Inside a packed auditorium, a tall, thin, slightly stooped man stands at the podium. At seventy-two years of age, Jean Vanier has a full head of white hair and deep-set eyes that exude warmth and wisdom. He is about to give his acceptance speech for the 2000 *Dignitas Humana* award, which each year honors individuals who serve the disadvantaged and marginalized in this world. Instead of the coat and tie one would expect at such an event, he is wearing a dark blue zippered jacket that looks like it came from the racks of a Goodwill thrift store. But somehow it seems just right as he begins to address his captivated audience in a simple and peaceful voice.

Finding a Life Path

Jean Vanier was born in Geneva, Switzerland, on Sept. 10, 1928, the son of the 19th Governor-General of Canada, George Phillas Vanier, and his wife, Pauline Archer Vanier. Both were devout Catholics, and sainthood causes for each have been launched in Canada. His father was also the Canadian ambassador to France at the end of World War II, where young Jean visited him in 1945 and saw men and women who had been liberated from the concentration camps. He later remembered, "They were skeletons. That vision has remained with me—what human beings can do to other human beings, how we can hurt and kill each other."

After a stint in the Royal Navy as a young man, Vanier joined a small community, *L'Eau Vive* (Living Water), made up mostly of students, in a poor area near Paris. Their goal was to foster prayer and reflection and they were directed by Father Thomas Philippe, a French Dominican.

Fr. Philippe went on to become chaplain of a small institution for men with developmental disabilities in the village of Trosly-Breuil, near Paris. His example inspired Vanier, who in 1964 decided to move to the same village and to buy a little, run-down house. He planned to form a kind of small family in the house with men who would otherwise languish in institutions.

A Heart and Home for the Broken

In preparing for this new "vocation," Vanier visited a number of institutions, asylums and psychiatric hospitals. He became keenly aware of the human tendency to shun people with odd behaviors or disabilities, to put them away and out of sight. He would later write:

> So many of us flee from people crying out in pain, people who are broken. We hide in a world of distraction and pleasure or in 'things to do.' We can even hide in various groups of prayer and spiritual exercises, not knowing that a light is shining in the poor, the weak, the lonely and the oppressed (*The Broken Body,* p. 1).

One easily finds reasons to "pass by on the opposite side" of the road when faced with people who are broken or in some way unattractive. Vanier did not do that. He took two mentally handicapped men into his home on Aug. 4, 1964. He called the home *l'Arche,* the Ark—after Noah's Ark—and this humble step marked the beginning of a movement that today encompasses a network of more than 130 homes around the world in which people with developmental disabilities live in a home with those who assist them. Together they share meals, household tasks, prayer, celebrations and sorrows, forming a family bond.

L'Arche's charter states that, in the Roman Catholic tradition, it "seeks to respond to the distress of those who are too often rejected, and to give them a valid place in society." The charter goes on to say that "everyone is of unique and sacred value" with a "right to friendship, to communion and to a spiritual life."

Friendship, the Deepest Need

In a world of great complexity, the vision of l'Arche is magnificent and touching in its simplicity. Reflecting on it now in his *Dignitas Humana* acceptance speech, Vanier says:

In L'Arche we live a sort of double mystery. There's the whole presence of Mary in Bethlehem and Nazareth, and Mary's standing at the foot of the cross. That has a lot of meaning for us, to stand and to be present and just to say "I'm with you, I'm with you."

In my own home there's a man named Patrick who, technically speaking, has a psychosis. And there's a lot of pain and a lot of anguish, in particular at some moments. But when I reflect about Patrick, he has everything he needs. He has good medication, good doctors. He has work, he works in the workshop. He has food, he has a home. But what does he need over and above that? He needs a friend. What is essential is somebody who believes in him, who trusts him, who sees in him a presence of God.

Who Is My Neighbor?

In 1983, a beautiful documentary titled "The Heart Has its Reasons" was filmed at the l'Arche home in Trosly-Breuil, featuring extensive footage of daily life in the home along with interviews with Vanier and the assistants. In one interview Vanier observes that there is a deep wound in the residents with developmental disabilities, a wound born of the feeling that they have failed their parents, disappointed their parents. The path toward healing lies in stable community and genuine friendship, rooted in the spirit of Christ and the Beatitudes.

Facing Our Poverty

Careful not to romanticize this experience, Jean Vanier recounts in his acceptance speech a sobering episode from community life in l'Arche.

> I remember when a man [an assistant] in one of our homes had been kept awake by one of the people who had screamed all night. He came to see me the next morning and he said, "You know, I wept all morning. I was in the chapel. I thought I could have killed him." We were talking about it, and I said to him, "You know, I think this is probably one of the most important days of your life. You came to L'Arche thinking you could do good to the poor, and you have. You've done a lot of good. But today you are discovering that you are poor. We all need help, and it's only as we discover that "I have

a handicap," that "I am broken," that "We're all broken," that we can begin to work at it.

At the conclusion of his speech, Jean Vanier receives a resounding ovation. There is applause that comes to speakers or performers because they are hugely entertaining. Then there is *this* applause, the kind that wells up from the depths of one's spirit, moved by the witness of a love that touches and transforms.

Postscript:

It is not surprising to learn that Jean Vanier became especially close to Pope John Paul II, who praised l'Arche as "a dynamic and providential sign of the civilization of love" and who chose Vanier to introduce the mysteries of the Rosary during his Papal pilgrimage to Lourdes in 2004. Less than two months before John Paul died in 2005, Vanier spoke lovingly of the ailing Pontiff in an interview on Vatican Radio:

> The Pope is a man who suffers. He suffers physically, but I also think he suffers enormously in his heart. And, at the same time, there is in him something that is extraordinarily luminous and limpid. The Pope is the sign of what Christianity is.... Today the Pope, more than with any encyclical, or any other writing, is a sign of holiness with his presence.

Who Is My Neighbor?

Pope Benedict XVI

[I]f in my life I fail completely to heed others, solely out of a desire to be "devout" and to perform my "religious duties," then my relationship with God will also grow arid. It becomes merely "proper," but loveless. Only my readiness to encounter my neighbor and to show him love makes me sensitive to God as well. Only if I serve my neighbor can my eyes be opened to what God does for me and how much he loves me.

(Encyclical *God is Love,* n. 18)

Love—*caritas*—will always prove necessary, even in the most just society. There is no ordering of the State so just that it can eliminate the need for a service of love. Whoever wants to eliminate love is preparing to eliminate man as such. There will always be suffering which cries out for consolation and help. There will always be loneliness. There will always be situations of material need where help in the form of concrete love of neighbor is indispensable. The State which would provide everything, absorbing everything into itself, would ultimately become a mere bureaucracy incapable of guaranteeing the very thing which the suffering person—every person—needs: namely, loving personal concern....

(ibid., n. 28)

The one who serves does not consider himself superior to the one served, however miserable his situation at the moment may be....Those who are in a position to help others will realize that in doing so they themselves receive help; being able to help others is no merit or achievement of their own. This duty is a grace....

(ibid., **n. 35)**

Questions for Discussion

1. Who stands out in your mind as a Good Samaritan in modern times? Feel free to mention famous people, but try also to think of examples closer to home.

   _____

   _____

   _____

   _____

   _____

   _____

2. In their quotes above, Pope John Paul II and Pope Benedict XVI indicate the personal qualities, the attitude and the approach of a true Good Samaritan. Discuss what those are.

_____

_____

_____

_____

_____

_____

_____

3. Those participating in this faith-sharing program are
    invited to be Good Samaritans through the service
    component. Have you thought about different ways
    you might give service, either individually or as a
    group? Discuss.

    _____

    _____

    _____

    _____

    _____

    _____

    _____

    _____

    _____

4. In a world that is often materialistic and "me-first," what can we do to help instill in our young people the spirit of the Good Samaritan?

_____

_____

_____

_____

_____

_____

_____

_____

5. In the last paragraph of his quote, Pope John Paul II points out one particular purpose of suffering in this world. Can you think of specific examples of human suffering that help demonstrate that he is right?

_____

_____

_____

_____

_____

_____

_____

6. What most impacted you from reading the account of
    Jean Vanier and l'Arche? Why?

    _____

    _____

    _____

    _____

    _____

    _____

    _____

Group Prayers of Intercession

8 to 10 minutes

Closing Prayer

Lord, make me an instrument of your peace.

> Where there is hatred,
> Let me sow love;

> Where there is injury, pardon;
> Where there is error, truth;

> Where there is doubt, faith;
> Where there is despair, hope;

> Where there is darkness, light;
> And where there is sadness, Joy.

O Divine Master, grant that I may not so much seek to be consoled, as to console;

To be understood, as to understand;

To be loved, as to love.

For it is in giving that we receive,

It is in pardoning that we are pardoned,

And it is in dying that we are born to eternal life.

Amen.

(Found written on a St. Francis of Assisi holy card in 1915 and piously but incorrectly attributed to him—author unknown)

Session 2

I Am the Vine, You Are the Branches

The Lord in His Scriptures

Jesus Reveals the Meaning of True Discipleship

"I am the true vine, and my Father is the vinedresser. Every branch of mine that bears no fruit, he takes away, and every branch that does bear fruit he prunes, that it may bear more fruit. You are already made clean by the word which I have spoken to you. Abide in me, and I in you. As the branch cannot bear fruit by itself, unless it abides in the vine, neither can you, unless you abide in me.

"I am the vine, you are the branches. He who abides in me, and I in him, he it is that bears much fruit, for apart from me you can do nothing. If a man does not abide in me, he is cast forth as a branch and withers; and the branches are gathered, thrown into the fire and burned. If you abide in me, and my words abide in you, ask whatever you will, and it shall be done for you. By this my Father is glorified, that you bear much fruit, and so prove to be my disciples.

"As the Father has loved me, so have I loved you; abide in my love. If you keep my commandments, you will abide in my love, just as I have kept my Father's commandments and abide in his love. These things I have spoken to you, that my joy may be in you, and that your joy may be full."
John 15:1-11.

Soak in the Word

Two Minutes of Silence

Reflect...

These words are spoken to the Apostles by Jesus at the Last Supper. It is his "farewell discourse," and he takes them deeper than ever before in their understanding of the intimate meaning of discipleship.

When he refers to himself as the "true vine," Jesus is drawing on familiar imagery. Grapevines were cultivated throughout Palestine, so their characteristics were well known. They required much pruning so that the plant's energies would go into producing grapes. When overgrown or barren branches were cut back, the discarded wood, too soft to be of any use, was gathered and thrown into a bonfire.

Many times the Old Testament prophets had referred to Israel, the Chosen People, as the vine or the vineyard of the Lord (see Isaiah 5:1-2; Jeremiah 2:21; Ezekiel 19:10; Hosea 10:1). Psalm 80 speaks of this in beautiful terms:

> Thou didst bring a vine out of Egypt;
> thou didst drive out the nations and plant it.
> Thou didst clear the ground for it;
> it took deep root and filled the land.
> The mountains were covered with its shade,
> the mighty cedars with its branches;
> it sent out its branches to the sea,
> and its shoots to the River (vv. 8-11).

And yet the prophets had been compelled to warn
Israel that in her repeated violations of the Covenant she
had become a wild and degenerate vine, fruitless and de-
serving of destruction (e.g., Isaiah 5:1-7). What would be
the remedy for this desperate situation? It would be the
coming of a "true" vine, Jesus Christ, source of the abun-
dant life and fruit of a New Covenant.

But there is an even deeper layer of meaning in this
imagery. Consider that Jesus' presentation of himself as
the vine comes nine chapters after he has presented himself as the Bread of Life (John 6:35-69). These images will
explode with meaning when at the Last Supper he holds
up the Passover *bread* and *wine* ("fruit of the vine") and
proclaims, "This is my body....This is my blood" (Mark
14:22,24).

The imagery takes us still further, since there is no
bread without the grinding of wheat, nor wine without the
crushing of grapes. And so it is that Jesus allows himself
to be ground and crushed in order to become for us the
Bread of Life and the Cup of Salvation. His life is totally
given, offered in fruitful sacrifice.

It is only by abiding in Christ the Vine that we too
can bear real fruit of love of God and neighbor. Jesus is
perfectly joined to the Father and offers himself on behalf
of all those the Father has sent him to save. *If we abide in
him he will prune and transform us so that our lives, too,
become an offering of love.* This is what we as disciples

must embrace and live. But on our own, without God's grace, we are incapable of it.

This is a challenging message, because the tendency of our fallen nature is to pride ourselves on personal achievement. We idolize the "self-made man." It is the American way. This is the exact opposite of the truth Jesus is calling us to recognize, the truth that without his grace we are barren and useless—but joined to him we are filled with his life, his love, his joy.

Catechism of the Catholic Church

787 - From the beginning, Jesus associated his disciples with his own life, revealed the mystery of the Kingdom to them, and gave them a share in his mission, joy, and sufferings.[1] Jesus spoke of a still more intimate communion between him and those who would follow him: "Abide in me, and I in you. . . . I am the vine, you are the branches."[2] And he proclaimed a mysterious and real communion between his own body and ours: "He who eats my flesh and drinks my blood abides in me, and I in him."[3]

---

[1] Cf. Mk 1:16-20; 3:13-19; Mt 13:10-17; Lk 10:17-20; 22:28-30.
[2] Jn 15:4-5.
[3] Jn 6:56.

Pope John Paul II

There cannot be two parallel lives in [the lay faithful's] existence: on the one hand, the so-called "spiritual" life, with its values and demands; and on the other, the so-called "secular" life, that is, life in a family, at work, in social relationships, in the responsibilities of public life and in culture. The branch, engrafted to the vine which is Christ, bears its fruit in every sphere of existence and activity. In fact, every area of the lay faithful's lives, as different as they are, enters into the plan of God, who desires that these very areas be the "places in time" where the love of Christ is revealed and realized for both the glory of the Father and service of others.

(The Lay Members of Christ's Faithful People, n. 59)

The Lord in the Life of His People

From Withered to Fruitful Branch: the Dorothy Day Story

Few figures have impacted the Catholic Church in America as powerfully as Dorothy Day. Founder of the Catholic Worker movement in 1933, she is remembered especially for her houses of hospitality for the poor and her social advocacy on their behalf. On Day's seventy-fifth birthday, Mother Teresa of Calcutta told her: "You have been such a beautiful branch on the Vine, Jesus, and allowed his Father, the Vinedresser, to prune you so often and so much. You have accepted all with great love." What follows is a brief look at that "pruning" and the fruit it bore.

Raised in a family in which "the name of God was never mentioned," Dorothy Day nonetheless felt "haunted by God" her whole life (Dorothy Day, *The Long Loneliness*, p. 11). She recalled that even in childhood that Divine haunting had a Catholic tinge:

> It was Mrs. Barrett who gave me my first impulse toward Catholicism. It was around ten o'clock in the morning that I went up to Kathryn's to call for her to come out and play. There was no one on the porch or in the kitchen...and thinking the children must be in the front room, I burst in and ran through the bedrooms.

In the front bedroom Mrs. Barrett was on her knees, saying her prayers. She turned to tell me that Kathryn and the children had all gone to the store and went on with her praying. And I felt a warm burst of love toward Mrs. Barrett that I have never forgotten, a feeling of gratitude and happiness that still warms my heart when I remember her. She had God, and there was beauty and joy in her life (Dorothy Day, *From Union Square to Rome,* p. 26).

A Radical Departure

A precocious girl with a great talent for writing (her father, John Day, was a journalist), Dorothy Day went off to college at the age of sixteen. She carried with her a keen social consciousness that had been shaped by long walks through the poor neighborhoods of South Chicago. An avid reader, she had also been drawn in a special way to books that shed light on the unjust conditions afflicting the poor.

Dorothy was a radical at heart, and as a college student being groomed by "progressive" professors with little regard for religion, she drifted away from her instinctive enthusiasm for God and became persuaded that Christianity just wasn't radical enough. "I felt that religion was something that I must ruthlessly cut out of my life.... For me Christ no longer walked the streets of this world. He

was two thousand years dead and new prophets had risen
to take his place" (*The Long Loneliness,* pp. 43, 46).

Dorothy moved to New York City at the age of 18,
working as a journalist for socialist newspapers and
cheering the Communist Revolution of 1917. She pro-
tested and picketed and went to jail in the interest of
various causes: opposition to the draft, support for labor
unions, support for women's right to vote. She socialized
with radical poets and playwrights and artists. She went
through failed love affairs, a marriage that lasted a year,
and an abortion she would regret for the rest of her life. A
friend committed suicide. Some biographers say Dorothy
herself attempted suicide when a man she had been living
with left her. Bright and talented as she was, her life was
a wreck.

Had God abandoned Dorothy? Left her in her confusion and sin? No, even in those darkest hours she felt the
prodding of his Spirit. She wrote:

> Many a morning after sitting all night in
> taverns...I went to an early morning Mass at St.
> Joseph's Church on Sixth Avenue and knelt in
> the back of the church, not knowing what was
> going on at the altar, but warmed and comforted
> by the lights and silence, the kneeling people and
> the atmosphere of worship (*ibid.,* p. 84).

"The Happiest Moment of My Life"

And so Dorothy continued in a swirl of contradictions. A turning point for her occurred when she became pregnant in the course of a common-law marriage to British atheist Forster Batterham. Because she had feared the earlier abortion had left her sterile, this pregnancy, illicit though it was, seemed to her a sign of grace and hope. The birth of little Tamar Teresa flooded her with renewed religious feeling. "No human creature could receive or contain so vast a flood of love and joy as I often felt after the birth of my child" she wrote. "With this came the need to worship, to adore" (*The Long Loneliness,* p. 139).

Dorothy resolved that Tamar would be baptized Catholic, though she knew this would drive Forster away (it did). Ultimately, she herself was received into the Church in December of 1927 and confirmed the following Pentecost. In an article in 1975 she recalled that Pentecost as "the happiest moment of my life."

Dorothy's love of Christ and the Church deepened day by day, but she wrestled with how the struggle for justice that ran so deep in her heart fit with her new life as a Catholic. She loved the saints (with a special devotion to St. Thérèse of Lisieux) and saw how much they had done to minister to the poor, the sick and the downtrodden. "But there was another question in my mind," she wrote.

"Why was so much done in remedying the evil instead of avoiding it in the first place? ...Where were the saints to try to change the social order, not just to minister to the slaves but to do away with slavery?" (*From Union Square to Rome,* p. 50).

The Catholic Worker Is Born

And so in 1932, on the feast of the Immaculate Conception, Dorothy poured out her heart to God at the National Shrine in Washington, D.C. She prayed that "some way would open up for me to use what talents I possessed for my fellow workers, for the poor" (*The Long Loneliness,* p. 166).

Her prayer was answered the very next day, when she met Peter Maurin, an immigrant from France and former Christian Brother, who shared with her a vision for joining Christian charity and holiness with the struggle for justice. Together they founded the *Catholic Worker* newspaper, aimed at changing society through the Church's social teachings, and in less than a year 100,000 copies were being printed each month. The newspaper spawned a movement attracting idealistic young men and women and leading to the establishment of houses of hospitality for the homeless and the hungry. Here at last was a radical Christian alternative to the Marxist agenda for the poor and the working class. It embraced charity and

pacifism, focusing on a revolution of hearts in the spirit
of the Beatitudes rather than armed class warfare. Today
there are close to 200 Catholic Worker houses throughout the world. They have always operated independently,
without officers or boards of directors, joined only by their
common vision rooted in the Gospel.

A Life Rooted in the Eucharist

Dorothy was an active contemplative. She understood
that she and those working with her could bear fruit only
if they were united as branches to Christ the Vine, and
that it would be better for the Catholic Worker movement to dissolve than for it to lose sight of that truth.
The center of her life was daily Mass and the Eucharist.
Many times she insisted to those who would join her in
the movement that the Mass was "the greatest work of
the day" and that all other works must flow from worship.
Her daily spiritual regimen included praying the Office
and the Rosary, meditating on Scripture and doing spiritual reading. She even considered leaving the Catholic
Worker movement for a more contemplative life in the
1940's, but ultimately decided against it.

Cause for Canonization Opens

Dorothy Day died on November 29, 1980. Just twenty
years later, on March 16, 2000, Cardinal John O'Connor
of New York announced with great joy that the opening

of her cause for canonization had been approved by the Vatican. This was especially fitting in that she had insisted often that every Christian is called to be a saint.

Let us conclude with one last quote from this great woman. It comes from a Christmas reflection on Mary and Joseph finding "no room" at the inn in Bethlehem:

It is no use to say that we are born two thousand years too late to give room to Christ. Nor will those who live at the end of the world have been born too late. Christ is always with us, always asking for room in our hearts.

But now it is with the voice of our contemporaries that He speaks, with the eyes of store clerks, factory workers and children that He gazes; with the hands of office workers, slum dwellers and suburban housewives that He gives. It is with the feet of soldiers and tramps that He walks, and with the heart of anyone in need that He longs for shelter. And giving shelter or food to anyone who asks for it, or needs it, is giving it to Christ *(Catholic Worker,* December, 1945).

Questions for Discussion

1. Jesus tells us we must abide in him and in his love
    in order to bear fruit. What are some of the keys to
    abiding in him? What have holy men and women like
    Dorothy Day done to deepen their abiding union with
    Christ?

    _____

    _____

    _____

    _____

    _____

    _____

2. Jesus talks about our need for "pruning" by the Father. How do you think that happens in our lives? How did it happen in the life of Dorothy Day?

_____

_____

_____

_____

_____

_____

_____

3. What differences exist between doing social work and
    charitable outreach simply for humanitarian reasons
    and doing it in such a way that we are motivated by
    Christ and see him in the persons we are serving?
    Think of as many differences as you can, from various
    perspectives (that of the giver, the receiver, an observ-
    er, even the whole Body of Christ).

    _____

    _____

    _____

    _____

    _____

    _____

    _____

    _____

4. Various biographers have argued that Dorothy Day's Christ-centered life and work cannot be stereotyped as either "liberal" or "conservative." Do you agree, and if so, why? What lessons does she teach us here?

_____

_____

_____

_____

_____

_____

_____

5. One of Dorothy Day's favorite quotations was spoken by the saintly Fr. Zossima in Dostoevsky's *The Brothers Karamazov:*

> "Love in practice is a harsh and dreadful thing compared to love in dreams."

What do you think this means?

_____

_____

_____

_____

_____

_____

_____

6. In the quotation from Pope John Paul II, he talks about the danger of separating our lives into two parallel dimensions—our "spiritual" life and our "secular" life.

    · What might be some examples of this?
    · Why do you think it happens so easily?
    · What can we do to avoid it?

_____

_____

_____

_____

_____

_____

_____

_____

Group Prayers of Intercession

8 to 10 minutes

Closing Prayer

Dorothy Day's Prayer for Love

Pray with me...
That men be joined together in love,
so strong a love in their march Godwards,
that they will draw all with them,
that all suspicion, anger, contention, bitterness
    and violence
be burnt away in the fire of this love.

And may it open their eyes,

the brightness of this love,

to the works we can all perform together

in building up a new society,

in our work for food, clothing, shelter, education

and health for all men.

For these are the works of mercy,

of love and not of hate,

the works of good, not evil,

of God, not the Devil,

and where there is no love, put love and we will
    find love;

because love is the measure by which we shall
    be judged.

Amen.

(*Catholic Worker,* January 1963)

Session 3

You Will Have Treasure in Heaven

The Lord in His Scriptures

Encounter with the Rich Young Man

And as he was setting out on his journey, a man ran up and knelt before him, and asked him, "Good Teacher, what must I do to inherit eternal life?"

And Jesus said to him, "Why do you call me good? No one is good but God alone. You know the commandments: 'Do not kill, Do not commit adultery, Do not steal, Do not bear false witness, Do not defraud, Honor your father and mother.'"

And he said to him, "Teacher, all these I have observed from my youth."

And Jesus looking upon him loved him, and said to him, "You lack one thing; go, sell what you have, and give to the poor, and you will have treasure in heaven; and come, follow me."

At that saying his countenance fell, and he went away sorrowful; for he had great possessions.

And Jesus looked around and said to his disciples, "How hard it will be for those who have riches to enter the kingdom of God!" And the disciples were amazed at his words. But Jesus said to them again, "Children, how hard it is to enter the kingdom of God! It is easier for a camel to go through the eye of a needle than for a rich man to enter the kingdom of God."

And they were exceedingly astonished, and said to him, "Then who can be saved?"

Jesus looked at them and said, "With men it is impossible, but not with God; for all things are possible with God."

Peter began to say to him, "Lo, we have left everything and followed you."

Jesus said, "Truly, I say to you, there is no one who has left house or brothers or sisters or mother or father or children or lands, for my sake and for the gospel, who will not receive a hundredfold now in this time, houses and brothers and sisters and mothers and children and lands, with persecutions, and in the age to come eternal life. But many that are first will be last, and the last first."
Mark 10:17-31.

Soak in the Word

Two Minutes of Silence

Reflect...

This encounter is described in all three Synoptic Gospels—Matthew, Mark and Luke—with slight variations. All three tell us the man was rich, Matthew tells us he was young, and Luke tells us he was a ruler (presumably a Jewish leader, perhaps in charge of a synagogue).

Mark's account of this meeting is especially vivid. Notice the eagerness of the young man. He *runs* to Jesus and *kneels* before him. He uses flattering words, calling out, "Good Teacher." Many times in the Gospels Jesus is called "Teacher" ("Rabbi" in Hebrew), but nowhere else is he called *"Good"* Teacher.

Of course, the young man speaks the truth in his flattery, but Jesus nonetheless challenges him: "Why do you call me good? No one is good but God alone." It is as if to say, "I rebuke your attempt to manipulate me through flattery, but in fact you speak a deep truth about who I am, a truth that you yourself do not understand."

The young man asks what he must do to inherit eternal life. Jesus begins with the basics—the Commandments. When the young man justifies himself as having kept all these, Jesus challenges him at a deeper level. Looking into the depths of his heart, Jesus knows exactly where the chains are, knows what needs to be purified and set free. He challenges him to let go of his wealth, to give it to the poor, and to come follow him as a disciple. Of course this would mean giving up not just riches, but the power and prestige that go with them.

Here Mark adds a beautiful detail: "Jesus looking upon him loved him."

You see, Jesus is not trying to trip the man up, or to make him squirm. He truly loves him, just as he loves each of us. He wants this earnest young man to let go of false riches in order that he might have "treasure in heaven." He wants him to find the peace and joy that are deep and lasting, not the surface happiness and prosperity that can be lost in an instant.

But the gaze of love is met by a downcast gaze of sadness, so Jesus turns his message immediately to his disciples. He uses the image of a camel trying to pass through the eye of a needle to express how hard it is for the rich to enter the kingdom of God. This makes his point powerfully, since the camel was the largest animal in Palestine.

Why are the disciples "astonished" at Jesus' words? One reason is that the Jews generally held to what we might call a "prosperity gospel," the belief that earthly wealth was to be sought and celebrated as a sign of God's approval and blessing. But here is Jesus turning this notion on its head, saying that God's special love is for the poor, for those who renounce the riches of this world.

Yet against all odds, God can still save the rich man. But for those willing to set aside everything to follow the Lord there will be an unimaginable abundance of blessings, mingled with a share in his Cross (see also John 15:18-21). In the world's eyes, the poor, humble followers of Christ may be insignificant fools, but the next life will reveal everyone's true colors.

What will it reveal about me?

Catechism of the Catholic Church

1723 - The beatitude we are promised confronts us with decisive moral choices. It invites us to purify our hearts of bad instincts and to seek the love of God above all else. It teaches us that true happiness is not found in riches or well-being, in human fame or power, or in any human achievement...but in God alone, the source of every good and of all love:

> All bow down before wealth. Wealth is that to which the multitude of men pay an instinctive homage. They measure happiness by wealth; and by wealth they measure respectability. . . . [1]

[1]John Henry Cardinal Newman, "Saintliness the Standard of Christian Principle," in *Discourses to Mixed Congregations* (London: Longmans, Green and Co., 1906) V, 89-90.

Pope John Paul II

"Jesus, looking upon him, loved him."

My wish for each of you is that you may discover this look of Christ, and experience it in all its depth. I do not know at what moment in your life. I think that it will happen when you need it most....

Man needs this loving look. He needs to know that he is loved, loved eternally and chosen from eternity. At the same time, this eternal love of divine election accompanies man during life as Christ's look of love. And perhaps most powerfully at the moment of trial, humiliation, persecution, defeat, when our humanity is as it were blotted out in the eyes of other people, insulted and trampled upon. At that moment the awareness that the Father has always loved us in his Son, that Christ always loves each of us, becomes a solid support for our whole human existence.

(Apostolic Letter to the Youth of the World, **on the Occasion of the 1985 International Year for Youth, n. 7)**

The Lord in the Life of His People

A Rich Young Man Who Followed

After reading about the rich young man who sadly walked away from our Lord, it is refreshing to learn of a young fellow born into wealth who radically embraced Christ's invitation. The son of a wealthy Italian publisher, Blessed Pier Giorgio Frassati found his greatest joy among the poor and the sick. The following article from Faith and Family *magazine has been edited slightly for this book.*

Pier Giorgio Frassati was born on April 6, 1901, to wealthy secularists in Turin, Italy. His mother was a painter, his father a prominent liberal journalist. Pier had trouble in school, failing test after test until he entered a Jesuit academy—where extra help got him through. Young Pier wasn't a "brain." He was far more interested in sports.

Athletic, handsome, and bounding with charisma, young Frassati gained a reputation as a practical joker. His pranks included short-sheeting priests' beds. He would sign letters to his friends as the murderous French revolutionary "Robespierre," adding the motto "Terror conquers all."

The Sinister Ones

Pier organized expeditions in the Alps for a band of boys he dubbed the *Sinistri* (the "Sinister Ones"), adopting the slogan: *Pochi ma buoni come macaroni* (roughly translated: "The Few, the Proud, the Macaroni"). Frassati led his Sinister Ones on arduous mountain-climbing expeditions, leading them in the Rosary as they ascended. He urged them upward with the cry: "Higher and higher—there you can hear the voice of Christ!" For every climber who prayed, Pier agreed to grease his boots (a nasty but necessary mountaineers' chore). The climb would be followed by a wild ski-race down the mountainside.

When he wasn't risking life and limb, Frassati enjoyed theaters, museums and the opera, delighting in Italian, Christian culture. Widely read, with literary flair, Pier engaged his friends in long, lively discussions about Jesus, Heaven and hell—enriched with passages he had memorized from Dante's Divine Comedy and St. Paul's letters.

Visiting Jesus in the Poor

Each day, Pier received Communion; many nights he spent sleepless in silent Adoration—with his skis at the ready for dawn adventures. Pier filled his life with little sacrifices for the poor, whom he saw every day.

When friends asked how he could stomach the smelly environs of Turin's slums, Pier said: "It's to Jesus I go. Jesus comes to me every morning in Holy Communion and I repay Him in a very small way by visiting the poor. All around the sick and all around the poor I see a special light which we do not have."

His frugal father gave Pier a small allowance—which the boy promptly passed on to the needy. This usually included his bus fare, reports Frassati's niece, Wanda Gawronska. "My grandfather was very stern about punctuality at meals, so Pier had to run all the way home, if he wanted to eat."

Pier would often skip family vacations so as not to leave behind his friends among the poor. When asked why he rode third class on trains, he would answer, smiling, "Because there is not a fourth." Although his father owned a major newspaper, *La Stampa,* Frassati studied to work as a mining engineer, so he could "serve Christ better among the miners."

As Domenico Bettinelli, Jr., writes: "When [Pier] was a child, a poor mother with a boy in tow came begging to the Frassati home. Pier Giorgio answered the door and, seeing the boy's shoeless feet, gave him his own shoes. At graduation, given the choice of money or a car, [Pier] chose the money and gave it to the poor.

"He obtained a room for an old woman evicted from her tenement, provided a bed for a consumptive invalid, and supported three children of a sick and grieving widow.... Only God knew of these charities; he never mentioned them to others" (from "Blessed Pier Giorgio Frassati—A Saint for the Youth of the Third Millennium," at www.bettnet.com).

Frassati didn't just dispense pocket money to the poor, reports Wanda Gawronska: "He would do everything for those families—carry coal on his back to them, find the men jobs, buy them all shoes. Above all he gave them himself."

Charity is Not Enough

Pier also acted to challenge the system that had neglected the poor. "Charity is not enough: we need social reform," he liked to say. In 1919, he entered the Catholic Student Federation and Catholic Action—two organizations that would soon be suppressed by Mussolini's regime. Frassati also joined Italy's pro-Catholic Popular Party. Later, Pier Giorgio helped found a Catholic daily newspaper, *Momento,* devoted to spreading Catholic social teaching.

Pier helped lead marches of Catholic youth—a dangerous task in the wild streets of 1920's Italy. The Catholics were attacked by leftist Reds, by the anti-clerical Royal Police, and then by Mussolini's blackshirts.

Frassati fought back in self-defense, landing several times in jail.

When his father's liberal politics antagonized Mussolini, Fascist "squadristi" raided the Frassati home. Pier single-handedly ejected the thugs and chased them down the street. Pier reassured his friends, "It is not those who suffer violence who should fear, but those who practice it. When God is with us, we do not need to be afraid."

Frassati used to say that "God gives us health so that we may serve the sick." He visited invalids in hospitals and at home, bringing medicine and food. In 1925, he contracted polio, which struck him swiftly. He would die in only five days, at the age of 24. As Pier lay on his deathbed, he handed his sister Luciana some pawn tickets to redeem for some poor people. His last note, written with a nearly paralyzed hand, concerned the Converso family, who depended on him to pay for shots.

A Short Life that Touched So Many

At Frassati's funeral, his family was shocked to see more than 1,000 mourners from Turin's lower classes. These poor, in turn, were amazed to discover the true identity of their long-time benefactor. As Frassati's story became well-known, it inspired Catholics across the world —including a young Polish student, Karol Woytjla, who would later become Pope John Paul II.

To this day, Frassati's body remains incorrupt: "When they opened Pier Giorgio's tomb in 1981, his body was perfectly preserved," recalled one witness. "He had a smile on his face and a rosary in his hands. It was like meeting him for the first time."

Pier Giorgio Frassati was not the son his worldly parents expected—nor was he the somber contemplative many Catholics expect in one called "blessed." Among the mildest of his adventurous habits was smoking a pipe. As the public announcement of his beatification was being prepared, some well-meaning devotees had the pipe air-brushed out of the official Vatican photo.

The truth is that the man Pope John Paul II beatified on May 20, 1990, calling him, "a man of the eight Beatitudes," was a pipe-smoker, prankster, daredevil, and lover of God.

It is hard to imagine that He did not approve.

("The Wild One: Blessed Pier Giorgio," by John Zmirak. Reprinted with permission from the February 2001 issue of Faith & Family—The Magazine of Catholic Living. *All rights reserved.)*

Questions for Discussion

1. In the Gospels, Jesus warns often against the haz-
    ards of material wealth (see, for example: Mark 4:19;
    Matthew 6:19-24; Luke 6:24; 12:15-34; 16:19-31). In
    Matthew 6:19-21, he urges his disciples to store up
    lasting treasure in heaven rather than fading treasure
    on earth and says, "Where your treasure is, there will
    your heart be also." As Christians we can see how
    valid this is, and yet we struggle with it. What is going
    on? Why is it so difficult?

    _____

    _____

    _____

    _____

    _____

    _____

2. When Jesus challenges the rich young man to "sell what you have, and give to the poor," his face falls and he goes away sad. Reflect on this sadness—what does it tell you (there may be more than one aspect or "layer" to it)?

_____

_____

_____

_____

_____

_____

_____

3. We don't know how the rich young man's life unfolded after this encounter—but is his sadness cause for a sliver of hope? Bear in mind that he must have seen the way Jesus looked at him with love. Remember that St. Peter experienced deep sadness regarding an even worse betrayal of Christ accompanied by a "look" from the Lord (see Luke 22:55-62), and consider how he turned out.

   - Let your imagination picture some possible scenarios for the rich young man (the quote from Pope John Paul II may be of help here, too).

_____

_____

_____

_____

_____

_____

_____

4. Notice that Jesus is not interested only in the young man being released from his attachment to riches. He wants this wealthy fellow to help the poor. Statistics have shown that the wealthier someone is, the less they tend to give to charity as a percentage of personal income. How do you explain this?

_____

_____

_____

_____

_____

_____

_____

5. There is a saying attributed to Ralph Waldo Emerson: "Sow a thought, and you reap an action; sow an action, and you reap a habit; sow a habit, and you reap a character; sow a character, and you reap a destiny." Discuss in a concrete way how these stages might unfold in the life of someone wanting to live a life detached from wealth and given to loving service (like Pier Giorgio Frassati...or, by God's grace, like you).

6. Pier Giorgio Frassati was deeply misunderstood by his own wealthy parents, who often expressed their disappointment to him that he was not choosing to follow their "sensible" path in life. And yet he experienced an incredible joy, proving the truth of Jesus' assurance that those willing to renounce the attractions of this world would receive a "hundredfold" not only in heaven, but even here in this world (along with persecutions). Discuss what must have been the sources of his joy.

_____

_____

_____

_____

_____

_____

_____

Group Prayers of Intercession

8 to 10 minutes

Closing Prayer

Lord Jesus, you proclaimed the poor blessed,
And warned us against anxiety about money and
material possessions.
You told us that if we seek first your kingdom
and righteousness,
We will be given all that we need in this world.

You not only preached poverty, but lived it,
Accepting birth in a humble stable and declaring,
"Foxes have holes, and birds of the air have nests;
but the Son of man has nowhere to lay his head."

Help me, I pray, to let go of all attachment to
material wealth and status,
And instead to embrace that holy poverty of spirit
Which clings to nothing but you.

Help me to live with an open hand and heart;
Open to share all that I am and all that I have with
others, especially those in need.
I ask this in your name, and through the grace of
your Spirit.

Amen.

Session 4

A Thirst So Deep

The Lord in His Scriptures

Jesus, Source of Living Water

Now when the Lord knew that the Pharisees had heard that Jesus was making and baptizing more disciples than John (although Jesus himself did not baptize, but only his disciples), he left Judea and departed again to Galilee. He had to pass through Samaria. So he came to a city of Samaria, called Sychar, near the field that Jacob gave to his son Joseph. Jacob's well was there, and so Jesus, wearied as he was with his journey, sat down beside the well. It was about the sixth hour.

There came a woman of Samaria to draw water. Jesus said to her, "Give me a drink." For his disciples had gone away into the city to buy food. The Samaritan woman said to him, "How is it that you, a Jew, ask a drink of me, a woman of Samaria?" For Jews have no dealings with Samaritans. Jesus answered her, "If you knew the gift of God, and who it is that is saying to you, 'Give me a drink,' you would have asked him, and he would have given you living water." The woman said to him, "Sir, you have nothing to draw with, and the well is deep; where do you get that living water? Are you greater than our father Jacob, who gave us the well, and drank from it himself, and his sons, and his cattle?" Jesus said to her, "Every one who drinks of this water will thirst again, but whoever drinks of the water that I shall give him will never thirst; the water that I shall give him will become in him a spring of water welling up to eternal life." The woman said to him, "Sir, give me this water, that I may not thirst, nor come here to draw."

Jesus said to her, "Go, call your husband, and come here." The woman answered him, "I have no husband." Jesus said to her, "You are right in saying, 'I have no husband'; for you have had five husbands, and he whom you now have is not your husband; this you said truly." The woman said to him, "Sir, I perceive that you are a prophet. Our fathers worshiped on this mountain; and you say that in Jerusalem is the place where men ought to worship." Jesus said to her, "Woman, believe me, the hour is coming when neither on this mountain nor in Jerusalem will you worship the Father. You worship what you do not know; we worship what we know, for salvation is from the Jews. But the hour is coming, and now is, when the true worshipers will worship the Father in spirit and truth, for such the Father seeks to worship him. God is spirit, and those who worship him must worship in spirit and truth."

The woman said to him, "I know that Messiah is coming (he who is called Christ); when he comes, he will show us all things." Jesus said to her, "I who speak to you am he." Just then his disciples came. They marveled that he was talking with a woman, but none said, "What do you wish?" or, "Why are you talking with her?"

So the woman left her water jar, and went away into the city, and said to the people, "Come, see a man who told me all that I ever did. Can this be the Christ?" They went out of the city and were coming to him.... Many

Samaritans from that city believed in him because of the woman's testimony, "He told me all that I ever did." So when the Samaritans came to him, they asked him to stay with them; and he stayed there two days. And many more believed because of his word. They said to the woman, "It is no longer because of your words that we believe, for we have heard for ourselves, and we know that this is indeed the Savior of the world."

John 4:1-30, 39-42

Soak in the Word

Two Minutes of Silence

Reflect...

The shocking impact of Jesus, a Jew, taking interest in a Samaritan should be evident from our earlier reflection on the parable of the Good Samaritan. But there is more to note here. Not only is this a Samaritan, but it is a woman, and in Jesus' day it was scandalous for a Jewish man to be seen speaking to a woman. Many men didn't even speak to their wives publicly. And this is a woman of bad reputation. That is probably why she has come alone to the well at noon ("the sixth hour"), in the heat of the day, rather than following the usual practice of coming early in the morning when the other women of the community would have been there.

But Jesus is not concerned with appearances, or what other people will think. He has come to respond to the profound thirst for God present (though sometimes obscured) deep within the human heart of man and woman, Jew and Samaritan, rich and poor, saint and sinner. Beneath the sinfulness of this woman who carries the public shame of having lived with six different men, Jesus sees a heart open and thirsting for a grace as yet undiscovered.

Is there a more powerful experience of human need than thirst? Certainly hunger is compelling, but anyone who has been incredibly thirsty, with parched lips on a hot day, knows that this is more desperate. Indeed, the classic picture of desperation turned to joy is the man wandering lost in the desert, with nothing to drink, until at last he comes upon an oasis.

The woman at the well finds that thirst-quenching oasis in Christ, so much so that she forgetfully leaves her water jar behind as she goes into the town to share the news of her amazing encounter.

The Old Testament author of Psalm 42 uses thirst as an image of longing for God: "As the deer longs for streams of water, so my soul longs for you, O God" (verse 1). And in his agony on the Cross, Jesus himself cries out, "I thirst" (Jn 19:28). Certainly he is suffering physical thirst as the end of his agony draws near, following the exhausting ordeal of carrying the Cross to Golgotha and the loss of so much blood. But his physical thirst is nothing compared to the thirst of his heart, of his spirit. He thirsts to redeem us and draw us near to him as willing disciples of divine love—indeed, as his Bride the Church.

Catechism of the Catholic Church

2560 - "If you knew the gift of God!"[1] The wonder of prayer is revealed beside the well where we come seeking water: there, Christ comes to meet every human being. It is he who first seeks us and asks us for a drink. Jesus thirsts; his asking arises from the depths of God's desire for us. Whether we realize it or not, prayer is the encounter of God's thirst with ours. God thirsts that we may thirst for him.[2]

---

[1] Jn 4:10.
[2] Cf. St. Augustine, *De diversis quaestionibus octoginta tribus* 64,4:PL 40,56.

The Lord in the Life of His People

Living Water in the midst of the Culture of Death

For two decades, Norma McCorvey was an icon for abortion rights. As "Jane Roe," she was the plaintiff in the 1973 U.S. Supreme Court decision Roe v. Wade that legalized abortion through all nine months of pregnancy. In the early 1990's she was working as marketing director of an abortion clinic in Dallas, Texas. No one would have predicted what happened next.

Norma McCorvey was tough, with an "in-your-face" attitude. As she put it, "I could out-cuss the most crass of men and women; I could out-drink many of the Dallas taverns' regulars; and I was known for my hot temper. When pro-lifers called me a murderer, I called them worse. When people held up signs of aborted fetuses, I spit in their face."

Norma had known very little love in her life. Born Norma Leah Nelson to an alcoholic, neglectful mother who had been on the verge of aborting her, and a Jehovah's Witness father, she grew up poor. Her parents divorced when she was thirteen and Norma left school after the ninth grade. At the age of fifteen she was sexually assaulted by a male relative. At sixteen she married a steel worker, Woody McCorvey, who beat her. Upon learning she was pregnant, Norma left him to return home to her mother, where she gave birth to a daughter, Melissa. Norma's mother took charge of raising Melissa and more or less banished Norma from the house. Norma then began a long struggle with drug and alcohol abuse, drifting between various jobs, including carnival barker, bartender and house cleaner. She was a lost soul, living on the margins of society.

Poster Child for Abortion

At the age of nineteen, Norma had an affair with a married coworker, and this resulted in a second pregnancy. She gave the child up for adoption. Pregnant a third time in 1973 and living in Dallas, Norma began contemplating an abortion, though it was illegal in Texas at that time. Two eager pro-abortion attorneys learned of her situation and grabbed hold of it to challenge Texas law. The case ultimately went to the U.S. Supreme Court, where it was decided by the infamous *Roe v. Wade* ruling, setting in motion the deaths of nearly 1.5 million unborn children each year in the U.S. since 1973.

Overnight, Norma had become an abortion rights symbol. But she could see that the radical Ivy League lawyers and feminists celebrating her cause didn't really care about her as a human being. They viewed her as lower-class, vulgar, embarrassing, and chose not to invite her to many appearances or marches. "They only needed a pregnant woman to use for their case, so they could get abortion legalized," she would later say. Ironically, she chose not to have the abortion, but gave birth to the baby and put it up for adoption. But she continued to advocate for abortion rights and ended up working at the Dallas clinic. She started drinking more to ease the pain of what she witnessed—the dismembered babies, the broken women, the hardened staff.

But alcohol was no answer to the depths of Norma McCorvey's thirst. Lost and alone in her parched desert of rejection, sin and sadness, Norma needed to drink from another source.

Won by Love

A pro-life group began an outreach of prayer and sidewalk counseling in front of the Dallas clinic. Norma was told by the abortionist to infiltrate the group and get to know them so she could see what they were up to. That felt too hypocritical, so Norma would sit on a bench and observe them. She couldn't help but note that "each time they came, they were always happy. I wondered why. No one was happy in the abortion clinic."

Norma was particularly touched by a bright-faced little girl named Emily, the daughter of one of the pro-lifers. The seven-year-old would often run up to Norma with a smile and give her a hug. One time a woman at the clinic tried intentionally to trip Emily. Norma told the woman to get off the property and said, "How can you be so mean to her? She's just a child for heavens sake." When the woman left, Emily said, "Miss Norma, then why are you letting them kill babies inside there?" Reflecting on this, Norma said, "She was only seven but so wise, and I didn't have an answer for her. I was beginning to see the irony of what I was doing."

Numerous times Emily invited Norma to come to church with her and her family. Norma kept putting her off, but later reflected that "the Holy Spirit, God's love for me, was seeking me through the love of other people. In particular, God was working through little Emily."

Finally one day Norma relented and joined the family for church. She remembered: "I was sitting there with Emily and her family when John 3:16 was read. I became hot and uncomfortable. Then the pastor asked if anyone there wanted to know Jesus. I raised my hand, went up to the altar, and on July 22, 1995, I accepted Jesus as my Lord and Savior. I walked out a new creation in Christ!"

Finding Home

A couple of years later, Norma began to have a recurring dream in which a voice said to her, "My child, you are to come home to me." She first wondered if the message referred to her death, and then it occurred to her that the voice could be the devil. So she called Fr. Frank Pavone, the national director of Priests for Life, with whom she had become friends. She asked him what to make of the message. He encouraged her to pray about it. "I continued to hear this message, and I felt someone tugging at my heart. Pondering the message one day, I asked, 'Lord, what does this mean?' The answer I received was, 'I want you to come home...to my Church.' Relieved and thankful, I answered, 'Oh, I can do that!' On August 17, 1998, I entered the Catholic Church. I received the Holy Eucharist and was confirmed by Father Frank Pavone."

On one occasion Norma McCorvey was taping a television interview with Fr. Pavone when she asked him to bless a metal object she was wearing around her neck. It had once been a "pro-choice" bracelet, but no longer. She had had it melted down and refashioned in the shape of a cross. How appropriate that cross, that sign of suffering, for Christ is put to death once more in every unborn child killed by abortion. Yet it was also a sign of the Living Water that flows even now from Jesus' open side, bathing poor sinners, quenching their thirst, restoring them to life.

Who Is My Neighbor?

Poem by Karol Wojtyla (Pope John Paul II)

Song of the Brightness of Water

From this depth—I came only to draw water
in a jug—so long ago, this brightness
still clings to my eyes—the perception I found,
and so much empty space, my own
reflected in the well.

Yet it is good. I can never take all of you
into me. Stay then as a mirror in the well.
Leaves and flowers remain, and each astonished gaze
brings them down
to my eyes transfixed more by light
than by sorrow.

—1950

(From *The Place Within: The Poetry of Pope John Paul II,*
translated by Jerzy Peterkiewicz, Random House, 1994)

This is not an easy poem by the thirty-year-old priest, Fr. Karol Wojtyla (later Pope John Paul II). But some aspects are fairly clear. Christ is the well. He has "depth" and "brightness" and "light," and acts as a "mirror." Reflecting the woman who comes to him, he reveals her to herself. In that reflection she sees that she is full of "empty space." There is a reference in the last line to "sorrow," which must be because of her emptiness and, presumably, her sin. But the bright light of Christ is what captures her gaze, and the wondrous brightness of his light is more powerful than her sorrow, takes her beyond her sorrow.

This certainly fits the experience of the woman in the Gospel account, and also that of Norma McCorvey. Both were brought to confront honestly the sin in their lives, and both were led from the pain of that reflection to the thirst-quenching power of Christ, the source of Living Water.

Questions for Discussion

1. In your experience, what do you see people thirsting for in life? What do you thirst for?

   _____

   _____

   _____

   _____

   _____

   _____

   _____

2. Do you believe that in every person on earth there is
    some level of longing or thirst for God? If so, why is
    that often not evident in people's lives?

_____

_____

_____

_____

_____

_____

_____

3. What helps people awaken to a thirst for God?

_____

_____

_____

_____

_____

_____

_____

_____

4. Jesus was not embarrassed or put off about reaching out to a social outcast—the Samaritan woman. What about you? What kinds of people are easily disregarded or avoided today, and what opportunities do you have to reach out to them?

_____

_____

_____

_____

_____

_____

_____

5. Serving others can be a source of joy in which, without even seeking it, we find our own thirst quenched. On the other hand, sometimes service seems to lead to "burnout." What approach helps to foster the former and avoid the latter?

6. In the life story of Norma McCorvey, little Emily obviously plays a crucial role. Why is she so effective in reaching Norma, and what lessons can we draw?

Group Prayers of Intercession
8 to 10 minutes

Closing Prayer

As the deer longs for streams of water, so my soul longs for you, O God. My being thirsts for God, the living God. When can I go and see the face of God?

My tears have been my food day and night, as they ask daily, "Where is your God?" Those times I recall as I pour out my soul...

Here deep calls to deep in the roar of your torrents. All your waves and breakers sweep over me.... I say to God, "My rock, why do you forget me?...."

Why are you downcast, my soul, why do you groan within me? Wait for God, whom I shall praise again, my savior and my God.

Psalm 42:2-4,8,10,12

Session 5

Unbind Him and Let Him Go

The Lord in His Scriptures

The Raising of Lazarus

Now a certain man was ill, Lazarus of Bethany, the village of Mary and her sister Martha. It was Mary who anointed the Lord with ointment and wiped his feet with her hair, whose brother Lazarus was ill. So the sisters sent to him, saying, "Lord, he whom you love is ill." But when Jesus heard it he said, "This illness is not unto death; it is for the glory of God, so that the Son of God may be glorified by means of it."

Now Jesus loved Martha and her sister and Lazarus. So when he heard that he was ill, he stayed two days longer in the place where he was. Then after this he said to the disciples, "Let us go into Judea again…. Our friend Lazarus has fallen asleep, but I go to awake him out of sleep." The disciples said to him, "Lord, if he has fallen asleep, he will recover." Now Jesus had spoken of his death, but they thought that he meant taking rest in sleep. Then Jesus told them plainly, "Lazarus is dead; and for your sake I am glad that I was not there, so that you may believe. But let us go to him."

Now when Jesus came, he found that Lazarus had already been in the tomb four days. Bethany was near Jerusalem, about two miles off, and many of the Jews had come to Martha and Mary to console them concerning their brother. When Martha heard that Jesus was coming, she went and met him, while Mary sat in the house. Martha said to Jesus, "Lord, if you had been here, my brother would not have died. And even now I know that whatever you ask from God, God will give you." Jesus said to her, "Your brother will rise again." Martha said to him, "I know that he will rise again in the resurrection at the last day." Jesus said to her, "I am the resurrection and the life; he who believes in me, though he die, yet shall he live, and whoever lives and believes in me shall never die. Do you believe this?"

She said to him, "Yes, Lord; I believe that you are the Christ, the Son of God, he who is coming into the world." When she had said this, she went and called her sister Mary, saying quietly, "The Teacher is here and is calling for you." And when she heard it, she rose quickly and went to him. Now Jesus had not yet come to the village, but was still in the place where Martha had met him.

When the Jews who were with her in the house, consoling her, saw Mary rise quickly and go out, they followed her, supposing that she was going to the tomb to weep there. Then Mary, when she came where Jesus was and saw him, fell at his feet, saying to him, "Lord, if you had been here, my brother would not have died." When Jesus saw her weeping, and the Jews who came with her also weeping, he was deeply moved in spirit and troubled; and he said, "Where have you laid him?" They said to him, "Lord, come and see." Jesus wept. So the Jews said, "See how he loved him!" But some of them said, "Could not he who opened the eyes of the blind man have kept this man from dying?"

Then Jesus, deeply moved again, came to the tomb; it was a cave, and a stone lay upon it. Jesus said, "Take away the stone." Martha, the sister of the dead man, said to him, "Lord, by this time there will be an odor, for he has been dead four days." Jesus said to her, "Did I not tell you that if you would believe you would see the glory of God?" So they took away the stone. And Jesus lifted up his eyes and said, "Father, I thank thee that thou hast heard me. I knew that thou hearest me always, but I have said this on account of the people standing by, that they may believe that thou didst send me." When he had said this, he cried with a loud voice, "Lazarus, come out."

The dead man came out, his hands and feet bound with bandages, and his face wrapped with a cloth. Jesus said to them, "Unbind him, and let him go."
John 11:1-44

Soak in the Word

Two Minutes of Silence

Reflect...

In the Gospel of John, this is the last of Jesus' miracles (or "signs," as John refers to them) leading up to his Passion, death and Resurrection.

In reflecting on this account, St. Augustine tries to identify the deeper meaning of the miracle. He sees the raising of Lazarus as an image of the Sacrament of Penance, which raises us from death in sin to Life in Christ. Reflecting on Jesus' summons—"Lazarus, come out" (in some translations, "come forth")—he writes:

> When you confess, you come forth. For what does "come forth" mean if not emerging from what is hidden, to be made manifest. But for you to confess is God's doing; he calls you with an urgent voice, by an extraordinary grace. And just as the dead man came out still bound, so you go to confession still guilty. In order that his sins be loosed, the Lord said to his ministers: "Unbind him and let him go." What you loose on earth will be loosed also in heaven (St Augustine, *In Ioann. Evang.,* 49, 24).

With his own history of sin followed by a radical conversion, St. Augustine knew this lesson intimately. He is probably reflecting on his own past when he compares the condition of a sinner to the foul odor of the corpse of which Martha speaks. Augustine is forever grateful to Christ for having rescued him from the stench of sin and the tomb of spiritual death.

We cannot conclude this reflection without noting one more thing in this Gospel account. At the sight of Martha and Mary's sorrow, and the sorrow of those around them, "Jesus wept."

We need to pause and really absorb this. Remember, this is the Son of God who has purposely delayed his visit so that a good friend would die and he could then use that tragedy to teach a holy lesson to the loved ones left behind. That could almost seem cold and calculating until we read those two little words: "Jesus wept."

Why did he weep? Why weep when you know that within moments your friend will be living and breathing again, at your command?

It was love that made him weep, love faced with the heartbreak of a world weighed down by suffering, sin and death. Recall the opening message sent to Jesus by Martha and Mary: "Lord, he whom you love is ill." These poignant words apply just as well to all of us. We must admit the painful truth—we are all ill, afflicted in body and soul. Physical and spiritual death and decay are a sad part of the fabric of this fallen world. At the same time, we are all loved, and that is why Jesus poured out his life on the Cross to raise us from the tomb. And in his heart—a heart not only divine, but human like ours—he has also wept for each one of us. That is an image we should not forget.

Catechism of the Catholic Church

654 ...[B]y his death, Christ liberates us from sin; by his Resurrection, he opens for us the way to a new life. This new life is above all justification that reinstates us in God's grace, "so that as Christ was raised from the dead by the glory of the Father, we too might walk in newness of life."[1]

---

[1]Rom 6:4; cf. 4:25.

Pope Benedict XVI

...[L]ordship over death does not impede Jesus from feeling sincere "compassion" for the sorrow of separation. Seeing Martha and Mary and those who had come to console them weeping, Jesus "was deeply moved in spirit and troubled," and lastly, "wept" (Jn 11: 33, 35). Christ's heart is divine-human: in him God and man meet perfectly, without separation and without confusion. He is the image, or rather, the incarnation of God who is love, mercy, paternal and maternal tenderness, of God who is Life.

(General Audience of March 9, 2008)

The Lord in the Life of His People

St. John Vianney: the Transforming Power of a Holy Priest

The deeper meaning of the raising of Lazarus is well illustrated in the life of St. John Vianney, who brought profound conversion to his little country parish in Ars, France, making it a pilgrimage site for the whole world. One of the Church's most celebrated saints, he was declared Universal Patron of Priests by Pope Benedict XVI and a focal point for the Year for Priests (June 2009 – June 2010).

In the gently rolling countryside of France, a young priest approaches on foot the tiny village parish to which he has been assigned. It is a cold and misty February day in 1818. As he reaches the outskirts of the town, Fr. John Marie Vianney pauses, dropping to his knees in the wet grass to pray.

Out of the Ashes of the Revolution

Not even twenty years have passed since the end of the French Revolution with its bloody persecution of the Church. Still fresh in Catholic memory are holy martyrs like the sixteen Carmelite nuns of Compiegne, who in 1794 had been beheaded one by one at the guillotine for refusing to renounce the "silliness and nonsense" of their faith in Christ. During this Reign of Terror priests had been hunted, church bells silenced, roadside shrines toppled and smashed. But the parents of John Marie Vianney were fearless in hiding priests, gathering their neighbors after dark for Masses by candlelight in village barns. This drama of holiness and courage in the midst of evil helped confirm in the heart of John Marie a vocation to the priesthood.

Yet no one expects greatness from this humble priest. He has barely made it through the seminary due to academic struggles, and he has no natural charisma. A fellow priest describes him as pale and thin, with timid and awkward movements. His cassock and shoes are old and worn, his voice high and shrill. The words of Isaiah 53 fit him perfectly: "There was in him no stately bearing to make us look at him, nor appearance that would attract us to him" (v. 2).

The Challenge of Ars

If that is not enough, he now finds himself assigned as Curé (from the Latin *cura,* or "care," referring to the care of souls) of the tiny, insignificant farming village of Ars, a cluster of about forty small clay houses on bad soil. Small as it is, Ars manages to support four taverns that are the center of its social life. As in most of France, the Revolution robbed the people of priests and religious education, and the effects are still being felt. The townspeople have become ignorant, indifferent, vulgar and worldly-minded. Their social life is marked by drinking, dancing

117

and pleasure-seeking. In Ars, the Christian faith is perhaps not dead, but it is certainly in critical condition.

In his June 16, 2009, letter proclaiming the Year for Priests, Pope Benedict XVI recalled the challenge facing the new Curé:

> He arrived in Ars, a village of 230 souls, warned by his Bishop beforehand that there he would find religious practice in a sorry state: "There is little love of God in that parish; you will be the one to put it there." As a result, he was deeply aware that he needed to go there to embody Christ's presence and to bear witness to his saving mercy: "[Lord,] grant me the conversion of my parish; I am willing to suffer whatever you wish, for my entire life!" With this prayer he entered upon his mission. The Curé devoted himself completely to his parish's conversion, setting before all else the Christian education of the people in his care.

The new Curé immediately gives himself the task of visiting every home, where he asks about the crops, the childen, the relatives, always concluding with some inspiring words about God and the Church. When he preaches, he begs the people to love God, to put aside sensuality, drinking and cursing, to make Sunday holy. He preaches with passion, even with tears.

One morning, well before dawn, a villager enters the church and finds Fr. Vianney prostrate before the tabernacle, begging the Lord for the conversion of Ars.

For Love of the Poor

The humble Curé embraces a life of poverty, emptying his rectory of nearly all its furnishings and sleeping on the floor, using a log of wood for a pillow. He fasts much, and his diet consists mostly of an occasional boiled potato. He has a special love for the poor. This was noted in an encyclical of Pope John XXIII in 1959, on the hundredth anniversary of the death of the Curé of Ars:

> "My secret"—he said—"is easy to learn. It can be summed up in these few words: give everything away and keep nothing for yourself." This detachment from external goods enabled him to offer the most devoted and touching care to the poor, especially those in his own parish. He was very kind and gentle toward them and embraced them with a sincere love...indeed with reverence. He warned that the needy were never to be spurned since a disregard for them would reach in turn to God. When beggars knocked at his door, he received them with love and was very happy to be able to say to them: "I am living in need myself; I am one of you."
> *(Sacerdotii Nostri Primordia, nn. 14, 15)*

Fr. Vianney's care for the poor extends to the founding of a free school for girls in 1824, to which he gives the name "Providence." To better care for orphans and girls from destitute families, it soon becomes a boarding school. Each day he teaches catechism and takes his evening meal there. Because it exists for the poor, it is his heart's delight.

Sharing the Mercy of God

But the greatest service of Fr. Vianney, the one that will characterize and dominate his life as a priest, is carried out in the confessional. God grants him the gift of special insight into the lives and needs of his penitents, and the fame of the holy Curé of Ars spreads. The last thirty years of his life he spends up to sixteen hours a day in the confessional until, in 1859, over 100,000 pilgrims travel to the tiny village from all over the world. In his letter proclaiming the Year for Priests, Pope Benedict XVI noted:

> The Curé of Ars dealt with different penitents in different ways. Those who came to his confessional drawn by a deep and humble longing for God's forgiveness found in him the encouragement to plunge into the "flood of divine mercy" which sweeps everything away by its vehemence. If someone was troubled by the thought

of his own frailty and inconstancy, and fearful of
sinning again, the Curé would unveil the mystery of God's love in these beautiful and touching
words: "The good Lord knows everything. Even
before you confess, he already knows that you
will sin again, yet he still forgives you. How great
is the love of our God: he *even forces himself
to forget the future,* so that he can grant us his
forgiveness!" But to those who made a lukewarm
and rather indifferent confession of sin, he clearly demonstrated by his own tears of pain how
"abominable" this attitude was: "I weep because
you don't weep," he would say.... He awakened
repentance in the hearts of the lukewarm by
forcing them to see God's own pain at their sins
reflected in the face of the priest who was their
confessor.

Not surprisingly, the people of Ars experienced a
radical spiritual transformation thanks to the years of
holy example, priestly ministry and countless prayers and
sacrifices of their holy Curé.

Much, much more could be said (and much has been
written) of this holy priest who by his complete self-sac-
rifice and loving priestly ministry "raised from the dead"
the village of Ars and touched the lives of countless others

throughout the world. Popularly declared a living saint in his own day, he remained utterly humble. When Napoleon III wanted to decorate him as a knight, he asked, "Is there any money attached to it for my poor?" Told no, he asked that the decoration be returned.

Fr. John Marie Vianney died in 1859 and was canonized in 1925 by Pope Pius XI, who declared him Patron of Parish Priests in 1929. In proclaiming the Year for Priests in June of 2009, Pope Benedict XVI extended his patronage to all priests.

Questions for Discussion

1. Martha and Mary expressed the wish that Jesus had come earlier so that their "brother would not have died." But of course Jesus was acting with a purpose.

   • What would have been different if Jesus had acted according to their wishes? What was gained by waiting?

   • What lesson(s) can we draw from this in light of the fact that our prayers sometimes aren't answered the way we'd like them to be?

   _____

   _____

   _____

   _____

   _____

   _____

   _____

2. Even though Jesus knows he is about to raise Lazarus from the dead, the sorrow and grief of the people at the tomb moves him to weep.

   • How easy or difficult is it for you to picture Jesus weeping? What impact does such an image have on you?

   • Do you share Jesus' compassion for those suffering from grief, from loss, from loneliness? How can you best love and serve them?

_____

_____

_____

_____

_____

_____

_____

3. Were you familiar with St. John Vianney before reading the brief account in this session?

   • What impacts you most about him?

   • Clearly he was a servant in every way, but what was his greatest service, and why?

   _____

   _____

   _____

   _____

   _____

   _____

   _____

4. After Lazarus comes out of the tomb, Jesus says to the stunned onlookers, "Untie him and let him go."

   • What are some of the ways today that people are held in bondage by harmful patterns or sin (in small ways as well as large), needing to be set free?

   • How can they (and we) be helped?

   _____

   _____

   _____

   _____

   _____

   _____

   _____

5. What are the characteristics or symptoms of a life that is spiritually dead? What are the signs or symptoms of a life that is spiritually alive in Christ?

_____

_____

_____

_____

_____

_____

_____

Group Prayers of Intercession

8 to 10 minutes

Closing Prayer

Prayer of St. John Vianney

I love You, O my God,
and my only desire is to love You
until the last breath of my life.

I love You, O my infinitely lovable God,
and I would rather die loving You,
than live without loving You.

I love You, Lord
and the only grace I ask is to love You eternally...

My God, if my tongue cannot say in every moment
that I love You,
I want my heart to repeat it to You as often as I
draw breath.

Amen.

Session 6

Whoever Loses His Life for My Sake

The Lord in His Scriptures

At the Presentation in the Temple, the Cross Foreshadowed

Simeon blessed them and said to Mary his mother, "Behold, this child is destined for the fall and rise of many in Israel, and to be a sign that will be contradicted (and you yourself a sword will pierce) so that the thoughts of many hearts may be revealed."[1]

Luke 2:34-35

---

[1]Taken from the New American Bible, copyright © 1991, 1986, 1970 Confraternity of Christian Doctrine, Inc., Washington, DC, and used by permission of the copyright owner. All Rights Reserved. No part of the New American Bible may be reproduced in any form without permission in writing from the copyright owner.

"If Any Man Would Come After Me, Let Him...Take up His Cross"

Jesus began to show his disciples that he must go to Jerusalem and suffer many things from the elders and chief priests and scribes, and be killed, and on the third day be raised. And Peter took him and began to rebuke him, saying, "God forbid, Lord! This shall never happen to you." But he turned and said to Peter, "Get behind me, Satan! You are a hindrance to me; for you are not on the side of God, but of men."

Then Jesus told his disciples, "If any man would come after me, let him deny himself and take up his cross and follow me. For whoever would save his life will lose it, and whoever loses his life for my sake will find it."
Matthew 16:21-25

"Into Thy Hands I Commit My Spirit"

And as they led [Jesus] away, they seized one Simon of Cyrene, who was coming in from the country, and laid on him the cross, to carry it behind Jesus.

Two others also, who were criminals, were led away to be put to death with him.

And when they came to the place which is called The Skull, there they crucified him, and the criminals, one on the right and one on the left. And Jesus said, "Father, forgive them; for they know not what they do." And they cast lots to divide his garments. And the people stood by, watching; but the rulers scoffed at him, saying, "He saved others; let him save himself, if he is the Christ of God, his Chosen One!" The soldiers also mocked him, coming up and offering him vinegar, and saying, "If you are the King of the Jews, save yourself!" There was also an inscription over him, "This is the King of the Jews."

It was now about the sixth hour, and there was dark-ness over the whole land until the ninth hour, while the sun's light failed; and the curtain of the temple was torn in two.

Then Jesus, crying with a loud voice, said, "Father, into thy hands I commit my spirit!" And having said this he breathed his last.

Luke 23:26,32-38;44-46

Soak in the Word

Two Minutes of Silence

Reflect...

The selected Gospel passages show that the Cross was a constant point of reference in the life of Jesus, from infancy (the Presentation in the Temple) to Calvary.

The passage from Matthew is classic, impetuous Peter. Moments before, he has affirmed his belief in Jesus as "the Messiah, the Son of the living God" (v. 16), and Jesus has declared him the rock upon which he will build his Church (v. 18). But it takes Peter no time at all to make a mess of things. He forcefully rejects Jesus' talk of suffering and dying. In doing so, he rejects the very heart of Jesus' mission, which is our salvation. He sides (even if unintentionally) with Satan, who would like to destroy that mission. Jesus needs Peter to understand that the redeeming Cross is the *only* path to life, and that every true disciple must be willing to follow the Lord in embracing that Cross.

Then there is Simon, a passerby from the North African city of Cyrene who is in Jerusalem for the Passover. Suddenly he finds himself ordered by the guards to help Jesus (who is probably unknown to him) carry the Cross. There is food for reflection here. We would all like to choose the size, weight, time and place of our crosses. But a true disciple is called to accept a share in the Lord's Cross according to his designs, not our own. In life and at the hour of death, we are called to echo Jesus' final cry: "Father, into your hands I commit My spirit."

Catechism of the Catholic Church

605 - At the end of the parable of the lost sheep Jesus recalled that God's love excludes no one: "So it is not the will of your Father who is in heaven that one of these little ones should perish."[2] ...The Church, following the apostles, teaches that Christ died for all men without exception: "There is not, never has been, and never will be a single human being for whom Christ did not suffer."[3]

---

[2] Mt 18:14.
[3] Council of Quiercy (853): DS 624; cf. 2 Cor 5:15; I Jn 2:2.

Pope John Paul II

Christ does not explain in the abstract the reasons for suffering, but before all else he says: "Follow me! Come! Take part through your suffering in this work of saving the world, a salvation achieved through my suffering! Through my Cross." Gradually, *as the individual takes up his cross,* spiritually uniting himself to the Cross of Christ, the salvific meaning of suffering is revealed before him. He does not discover this meaning at his own human level, but at the level of the suffering of Christ....

A source of joy is found in the *overcoming of the sense of the uselessness of suffering....* Faith in sharing in the suffering of Christ brings with it the interior certainty that the suffering person...*is serving,* like Christ, *the salvation of his brothers and sisters.* Therefore he is carrying out an irreplaceable service. In the Body of Christ, which is ceaselessly born of the Cross of the Redeemer...it is suffering, more than anything else, which clears the way for the grace which transforms human souls. Suffering, more than anything else, makes present in the history of humanity the powers of the Redemption.

(On the Christian Meaning of Human Suffering, **nn. 26, 27)**

The Lord in the Life of His People

A Daughter of Israel Embraces Christ and His Cross

A woman, a Jew, a Catholic, an intellectual, a contemplative nun, a martyr. Edith Stein was all of these things. More than anything, she was a faithful disciple. She gave herself with utter generosity to Christ her Bridegroom and to her brothers and sisters, for whom she was willing to sacrifice, to suffer, and even to die.

> Let us put our hands in those of the Divine Babe, let us say our Yes to his invitation 'Follow me,' and we will be his. The way will be clear for his divine life to become incarnate in us. It is precisely this that is the light come through the darkness, a light kindled in the soul, the miracle of Christmas…. But upon the same light, shining so brilliantly in the manger, comes the shadow of the Cross. The road leads irresistibly from Bethlehem to Golgotha, from the manger to the Cross.

These words are from a lecture given by Edith Stein when she was 39 years old. They show a maturity attained through suffering. Born into a Jewish family on Yom Kippur, or the Feast of the Atonement, on October 12, 1891, she had grown up without her father, who died when she was two. Four of her ten brothers and sisters had died before she was born (she was the youngest). Moreover, she lived through a period of great conflict.

World War I erupted when she was in her twenties, and the Naziism of her native Germany would devastate the Jews twenty years later.

A Loving and Brilliant Daughter

From an early age it was clear Edith had a brilliant mind. Halfway through kindergarten, it was decided she would enroll in the first grade, though she couldn't read or write. She finished the year near the top of her class, often exasperating her classmates, one of whom exclaimed: "Oh, for once, let me be right!" It is not so much that she was proud as that she was simply a genius.

Edith had a special love for her mother, Auguste, a strong, virtuous woman who had to run the lumber business her deceased husband had left behind, even as she raised seven children. Though the photos we have of Edith show a rather somber face, she was in fact witty and amiable, made friends easily, and liked to play tennis and to dance. She was also strong-willed and independent, and though her mother was a devout Jew, Edith lost her faith and chose to stop praying at the tender age of fourteen.

At twenty, Edith began her university studies in her home town of Breslau, but a love of philosophy carried her to the University of Gottingen, where she studied under the great philosopher Edmund Husserl and even became his teaching assistant. Edith wanted to obtain a professorship, a goal that was impossible for a woman at the time. Still, Husserl wrote: "Should academic careers be opened up to women, then I can recommend her whole-heartedly and as my first choice for admission to a profes-sorship." All her life, Edith Stein would be a pioneer in witnessing to the gifts and capabilities of women.

The Light of Jesus Christ in the Mystery of the Cross

Edith noticed that Husserl's approach to philosophy often led other professors and students to Christianity (in fact, his "phenomenology" would greatly influence Pope John Paul II). In late 1917, one of Edith's professors and close friends, Adolf Reinach, was killed in the war. He and his wife Anna had been married less than five years and were Jewish converts to Christianity. When it came time for Edith to visit Anna, she feared she would find the young widow completely fallen apart. How surprised she was to see her instead sustained by serenity in Christ and hope in the resurrection. Edith wrote:

> It was my first encounter with the Cross, with this divine force that it confers on those who bear it. For the first time, the Church, born of the Passion of Christ and victorious over death, appeared clearly to me. At this very moment, my unbelief gave way, Judaism grew pale to my eyes, while the light of Jesus Christ rose in my heart—the light of Jesus Christ grasped in the mystery of the Cross *(Spiritual Works,* pp. 55-56).

"This is the Truth"

Edith's conversion was sealed in the summer of 1921, when she was vacationing at the estate of a Christian couple. One evening she noticed a copy of the autobiography of St. Teresa of Avila and picked it up. She didn't stop reading till dawn. She later wrote, "When I had finished the book, I said to myself: This is the truth."

Edith Stein received Catholic baptism on January 1, 1922. Ironically, she felt closer to her Jewish roots as a result. "I had given up practicing my Jewish religion when I was a 14-year-old girl and did not begin to feel Jewish again until I had returned to God." She now felt a sense of belonging to Christ not only spiritually, but also through her blood.

Edith's conversion to Catholicism devastated her mother, bringing about a painful rift between the two that would remain to her mother's dying day. This was compounded when, after several years of brilliant teaching, writing and lecturing as a Catholic philosopher, Edith finally followed what had become her heart's desire—to become a contemplative Carmelite nun. She entered the Carmelite Convent of Cologne on October 14, 1934, taking the name Teresa Benedicta of the Cross.

The Most Painful Cross

Two days earlier, on her birthday, Edith had gone to Breslau to say goodbye to her mother. It was the last day of the Feast of Tabernacles and the two went together to the synagogue. That evening her mother wept and wept. Edith held her in her arms, pressing the old white head to her breast for the longest time. When it became quite late, she helped her undress and sat on the bed to be near her, until her mother ordered her to get some rest herself.

The rift with her mother was Edith's most painful cross, but at a deep level she was at peace. Reflecting on the course of her life, she would write:

> Things were in God's plan which I had not planned at all. I am coming to the living faith and conviction that—from God's point of view— nothing is by chance and the whole of my life, down to every detail, has been mapped out in God's divine providence and makes complete and perfect sense in God's all-seeing eyes.

Holocaust

By 1938 the Nazis' hatred and persecution of the Jews had been fully unleashed and even a Catholic nun of Jewish heritage was not safe. Edith was smuggled across the border to a convent in the Netherlands. She composed her will there, writing:

> Even now I accept the death that God has prepared for me in complete submission and with joy as being his most holy will for me. I ask the Lord to accept my life and my death...so that the Lord will be accepted by His people and that His Kingdom may come in glory, for the salvation of Germany and the peace of the world.

The Germans invaded the Netherlands in 1940. In 1941, Edith wrote to a friend: "One can only gain a knowledge of the Cross if one has thoroughly experienced the Cross. I have been convinced of this from the first moment onwards and have said with all my heart: 'Ave, Crux, Spes Unica' ('I welcome you, Cross, our only hope')."

Edith and her sister Rosa, who had converted to Catholicism and come to serve at the convent, were arrested by the Gestapo on August 2, 1942 while the nuns were in chapel. Edith turned to Rosa and said, "Come, let us go for our people." The two sisters were sent briefly to transitional camps, before being put to death in the gas chambers of Auschwitz.

"Here is Someone Truly Great"

A survivor of Westerbork, one of the transitional camps, recalled Edith vividly. He noticed that many of the women in the camp simply fell apart when they arrived and could not care for their children. He wrote:

> It was Edith Stein's complete calm and self-possession that marked her out from the rest of the prisoners.... Many of the mothers were on the brink of insanity and had sat moaning for days, without giving any thought to their children. Edith Stein immediately set about taking care of these little ones. She washed them, combed their hair and tried to make sure they were fed and cared for. (Waltraud Herbstrith, *Edith Stein: A Biography,* p. 105)

From Westerbork, Edith was able to send back a pressing message to the nuns at her convent: "... [We] place our trust in your prayers. There are so many persons here in need of a little comfort, and they expect it from the sisters. (Letter 342 to Mother Ambrosia A. Engleman, 8 August 1912).

As she embraced the Cross, Edith poured herself out for others, holding nothing back for herself. A Dutch official who spoke with her at Westerbork recalled:

> I knew: here is someone truly great. For a couple of days she lived in that hellhole, walking, talking and praying...like a saint. And she really was one. That is the only fitting way to describe this middle-aged woman who struck everyone as so young, who was so whole and honest and genuine.

> At one point she said to me, "I never knew people could actually be like this...and I honestly had no idea of how my brothers and sisters were being made to suffer...I pray for them continually." ...[T]hen I saw her go off to the train with her sister [Rosa], praying as she went, and smiling the smile of unbroken resolve that accompanied her to Auschwitz. (Herbstrith, pp. 107-108)

Questions for Discussion

1. The first Scripture passage in this session shows
    Christ's Cross hinted at already at his Presentation in
    the Temple, in the prophecy of Simeon. In her opening
    quote, Edith Stein also sees the shadow of the Cross
    already present from the time of Jesus' birth in Beth-
    lehem.

    •   Some might say that associating the theme of
        the Cross with the Christmas season in any way
        is too morbid and grim, that it ruins that fes-
        tive celebration full of carols and lights and joy.
        Reflect and discuss.

    _____

    _____

    _____

    _____

    _____

    _____

2. The meaning of suffering, of the Cross, is a great mystery—difficult and painful to understand.

   • Does the quote from Pope John Paul II help to explain it in some way? Try to summarize what he is saying.

   • We all need to hear the Pope's message. But who in this world of ours is in most urgent need of it, and why?

   _____

   _____

   _____

   _____

   _____

   _____

   _____

   _____

3. In what ways and on what levels did Edith Stein give of herself in loving service? Consider even some of the smaller details.

_____

_____

_____

_____

_____

_____

_____

4. This session is the last in this set of meetings us-
    ing the book *Who Is My Neighbor*. What fruits, what
    benefits are you finding from this kind of faith-sharing
    experience?

---

5. Edith Stein was a brilliant person, an "intellectual."
   Some would argue that high intelligence is an advan-
   tage in terms of embracing a life of faith as a disciple
   of Christ. Others might argue that it can actually be
   a disadvantage. Think about it from different angles
   and discuss.

   _____

   _____

   _____

   _____

   _____

   _____

   _____

6. Simon of Cyrene is mentioned in all three of the
    Synoptic Gospels (Matthew, Mark and Luke). Even
    though extremely little is said about him, he has been
    immortalized in the Fifth Station of the Cross and
    featured prominently in films about the Passion of
    Christ (think of Mel Gibson's film, for example). Why
    does he hold such fascination, and what lesson(s) do
    you think God might want us to draw from his part in
    the drama?

    _____

    _____

    _____

    _____

    _____

    _____

    _____

    _____

Group Prayers of Intercession

8 to 10 minutes

Closing Prayer

O my God,

fill my soul with holy joy,

courage and strength,

to serve You.

Enkindle Your love in me

and then walk with me

along the next stretch

of road before me.

I do not see very far ahead,

but when I have arrived

where the horizon now closes down,

a new prospect will open before me,

and I shall meet it with peace.

Amen.

Prayer of St. Teresa Benedicta of the Cross (Edith Stein)

Appendix

Suggestions for Service

As stated in the Introduction, we are not truly disciples of Christ until we take seriously his words: "Truly, I say to you, as you did it to one of the least of these my brethren, you did it to me" (Matthew 25:40).

With a smile and an open heart, we are called to be the hands and feet of Christ in the world, especially to those in need. But sometimes we need a little help getting started. Here are a few suggestions:

Ask your pastor about needs in the parish community—

"Charity begins at home," and in the life of the Church that's your parish. Your pastor can help you learn who are the lonely, the elderly, the sick or homebound in your community. He can tell you who needs Holy Communion, the human kindness of a visit, and who has material needs. You might also ask if there are parishioners who need a ride to Mass because of age, health, or special needs.

Contact Catholic Charities—

Consider offering some volunteer time

to Catholic Charities, which has agencies throughout the country. To find one near you, visit **www.catholiccharitiesusa.org,** click on "Who We Are" and then "Local Agency Directory."

Check your Yellow Pages listings under "Social Service Organizations" or "Volunteer Services"—

You may be surprised to learn how many opportunities for service exist in your community: Meals on Wheels, Habitat for Humanity, Birthright or other crisis pregnancy centers, food pantries, homeless shelters, Catholic Worker houses, and more.

Pay attention to what is "right under your nose"—

Sometimes we can get tied up in a knot trying to decide where to go and what to do, when there's an elderly neighbor next door or a nursing home a few blocks away. No doubt, there are people close by that are lonely and would love a visit.

May the ancient witness be renewed:
"See how they love one another!"

Notes

Notes

Notes

Notes

Notes

Notes

The Discipleship Series

Novo Millennio Press